# OM

# THE UNIVERSE

# AND

# I

A Poetry Collection

By

Omer Toledano

~

For my parents

Hanna & Ehud Toledano

~

# Table of Contents

~

# The Pure Infant

by

Omer Toledano

It has become contaminated
Trying to push back the dirt
I cleanse myself
Almost like an infant
On the day of its birth
Not a spec of dust
Or pollution
Clean
Pure
No past
Just dirt awaiting to latch on
I re-awaken
Only to find pollution
And I weep silently
Like a baby

I long to find my way again

To be in the place

To be pure

To be timeless

Without a spec of dust

Without the dirt

Thrust upon me by time

There I remain

For you

To come back

~

# The Void

by

Omer Toledano

In the void between sound

Two worlds collided

They danced and they swirled

Together abided

Primordial rhythm

Was the path unto them

And within it the rock

Which was to be their gem

In what seemed like a year

Will last for a lifetime

Throughout eons will echo

As we hear the night chime

It will arise and subside

As this wave always has

And continue this play

This sonic of jazz

In the void between worlds

There is nothing to see

There is nothing to hear

There is nowhere to be

You know it is there

And you know it is not

It is just in between

Where you seem to be caught

It will come it will go

And what you need to know

You will find out through time

And in time it will show

What needs to be shown

And to you will appear

Could be space

Could be time

Or the one you hold dear

In the void is where you
Feel most comfortable being
Where you talk with yourself
Where you're actually seeing
Out there is just show
They are not in the know
Of the things that are real
And which help you to grow

I am that I am
I am bliss overjoyed
I am truth I am found
In this infinite void

~

# Expectation

by

Omer Toledano


It's my past which has shown me

What to expect

In this way which I live

I must pass

And reject

In this way which they live

They come to expect

What should be

Must be done

And how one must act

In this way how they judge

And draw their conclusion

Based on lies

Not the truth

Just their simple delusion

It's how they are built

It's how they are wired

So you know if you're in

So you know if you're hired

And this is the essence

Of this grand design

Are you with him?

Or are you still mine?

Either way it won't matter

The answer you know

As for I with the truth

Of you I let go

And continue to do so

Time after time

And write poems about it

Rhyme after rhyme

~

# The Voices

by

Omer Toledano

The voices keep telling me

That I know nothing of love

It tells me to stay away

That I do not belong in this realm

Every fiber in my being says "Don't do this!"

"Go home! Relieve yourself."

The voice tells me that it is true

It is not for me

It is a mess

Even the strongest like yourself

Fail to keep balance

One big delusion created

To maintain momentum

Perpetuation

To keep the wheel in motion

It is not for you

Sit in the back seat

And enjoy the scenery

~

# The Formless Rabbit

by

Omer Toledano

Once there was a formless rabbit
Who liked routine, order and habit
Every morning went on foot
And pulled a carrot from the root
And this went on for quite a while
This was just the rabbit's style
And so one day, the rabbit woke
And saw this thing was quite a joke
Pulling carrots from the ground
To and fro without a sound
And so the rabbit did agree
That eating carrots should be free
No more effort to this deed
Just the planting of a seed

And so the rabbit thought and thought
Of everything that he'd been taught
And then it came in quite a flash
The rabbit knew what he must do
To whip another by the lash
And so the rabbit brought his friend
To pick his carrots till the end
But now the rabbit reigned supreme
Alone atop this corrupt scheme
And this continued till the end
Our formless rabbit did not bend
Wanted just to move ahead
Blind to all as light of day
Pushing sideways on the way
And finally when he had topped
Breathed his last breath
And to death he dropped

But formless rabbit was not done
For now he was with nature one
And quicker than he knew what hit him
Faster than his lifeless rhythm
He looked around
Began to stare
Formless rabbit was now a bear

~

# Miracle of the Tow Cable

by

Omer Toledano

In the darkness of night
A voice whispers
"I am here with you, always"
Remember the miracle of the tow cable
You entered the clearing in the forest
And when you needed it
It was there on the ground
With no earthly business being there
Put your faith in what your eyes see
I put it there for you
I pulled you out of where you were
And I shall do so many more times over
My hand guides your path
Trust the process
Remember the miracle of the tow cable

~

# Queen of the Aztecs

by

Omer Toledano

I'm the autumn, you're the spring
I'm the rain, you're the blossom
I'm a bird in mid flight
You're the flower in my sight

Yours the people of the sun
Mine the people of the moon
Both the people of the light
Both illuminating noon

Darkness chaos with no end
Has no place in our domain
No fear, suffering or pain
Only love and joy will reign

Identify the falls we must

To hasten cure in both we trust

And do what is forever right

You illuminating day

And I illuminating night

Epitome of all desire

You're my ice

You're my fire

My wings with you shall never tire

With you, my love, a frequent flyer


And hosts of heaven and the earth

Will gaze upon as we give birth

To all that was and that will be

They'll give their blessing

You and Me

I will promise here on end
To cherish, keep you and defend
With music sounding when you wake
And whisper when a dream you make
My heart is here for you to take
Like the still waters on a lake

You're the mission in my eye
You're the pinnacle so high
You're the prize which I have won
Sun and Moon
Together One

~

# The Dead Sea Hotel

by

Omer Toledano


One morning she asked
If I want to come with her
Just her and myself
And her son and her sister

Happily I inclined
And accepted the charge
Didn't flinch didn't waver
Was as they say, large

I booked me a room
At the Dead Sea Hotel
What transpired thereafter
Nobody could tell

I bathed and I soaked

Down in the spa

Got a healthy massage

From an elderly ma

We had dinner and fun

In the Bedouin tent

I had chicken skewers

And I was content

After filling our bellies

We went and retired

Night was falling

And we were all tired

And as we were sitting

Alone in the room

Her face suddenly dropped

And I sensed the gloom

She told me that she

No longer felt well

With us

Here

At the Dead Sea Hotel

And more things were said

And as I lay there in bed

I thought and I wondered

What went on in that head

The sun rose next morning
And the place was so calm
The mountains, the air
And the sand on my palm
If only I thought
She could be here
Right now
Instead of thinking the what
The when and the how

And again on the terrace
Looking out from above
She was absent from this
And from that and from love
It was there that I kissed her
Just our lips were aligned
Only looking at her
She was not of sound mind

On the drive back to home

Nothing could be done

The verdict already passed

And in there it was gone

With her beautiful eyes

I could already tell

She left me once more

At the Dead Sea Hotel

~

# The Silent Ceremony

by

Omer Toledano


On the Greek island of Rhodes

I looked at the waves crashing down on a pebble beach

The city on my right

The sun and you on my left

The Turkish mountains on the horizon

I looked at the mildly turbulent sea

And then I looked into your eyes and saw the storm within

I looked back at the waves

And back at you

Your hair fluttering in the cool evening breeze

Your eyes piercing into my soul

The love of my life

Then back at the waves

Then back at you

Not a word was said

A silent ceremony

And that was the beginning of summer

~

# His Heart Beats Only for You

by

Omer Toledano

Nothing can be done about it

The more he thought about it

The more he tried in vain to change the tune

To change the rhythm

On His schedule there is no other

Violins playing a familiar song

Of a man who once was and is no more

Whose heart beats only for you

It's all that is left of this poor soul

Just a heart and it beats only for you

It is all crystal clear

How a month passes, then a year

How he once whispered in your ear

All the things that you wanted to hear

Promises left with a tear

To flow on his cheek as the violins played

He is hurt, he is wounded

Like an animal left to gasp his last breath

To welcome death

To come and take him for he cannot go on living

For he knows that once there were two

And his heart beats only for you

~

# Where Does the Wikipedian Fall?

by

Omer Toledano

The sky up above

The Earth down below

The valley runs deep

The river does flow

The flower in bloom

And this tree grows so tall

As he gazed out at them

He kept asking himself

Where does the Wikipedian fall?

And to every astronomer

And author a name

And to every king in existence

Whom the throne did he claim

To every painting and artist
With a place down the hall
He asked with a sigh
Where does the Wikipedian fall?
To every event that was dreary
And physical theory
Every book that was sold
And places so eery
Every music and lyric
Known to man's ears
Birds of the heavens
And bison and deers
And historical facts
And post-war pacts
And fictional figures
And theatrical acts

From the Hollywood sign

To China's Great Wall

He asked once again

Where does the Wikipedian fall?

And despite all he's done

He really did love it

Like the Gurus he followed

He was from the world

But not of it

He knew for a fact

That his knowledge was small

As that old man once said

We can't harness it all

He bears silent witness

As he answers the call

And continues to ask to this day

Where does the Wikipedian fall?

~

# The Rosetta Stone

by

Omer Toledano


I am the one
Who holds it together
I am the master
In charge of the tether

I am the one
Entrusted with power
I am the one
Who holds up the tower

If it wasn't for I
It would all fall apart
If it wasn't for I
With the purple heart

Where they die all of them
The shy and the weak
Is where I come in
To combat the bleak
It takes courage to talk
It takes courage to walk
It takes courage to fight
And to hunt like a hawk

If I fall
They fall with me
And that cannot be
With their light and their goodness
They encircle me
So that one day I'd rise
And shield them from harm
But till then I bestow
Upon them my charm

I am the one
Who need not atone
I am the one
Who sets the tone
I am the one
I'm flesh and I'm bone
I am the only
Rosetta Stone

~

# Collective Orgasm

by

Omer Toledano


Does the amoeba feel pleasure

When it multiplies

Does the tiny fungus gasp

When it releases its tiny spores

Does the flower get aroused

When the bee suckles the nectar while touching its anthers

Does the tree sway in ecstasy

Before bearing fruit

In the words of the song

How does the spring know its time?

Does the mountain lion question anything

Before it mounts

Give and take

Take and give

Releasing excess

Recyclers of the universe we are

Taking in and spewing out

Magnificent creation

A brief enjoyable moment

A collective orgasm

In eternity

~

# The Water Knows

By

Omer Toledano


When you're there in the water
It's a fresh cool sensation
It cleans you of all
Removes condensation
In this liquid you're free
It's all relaxation
You're stripped of your worries
You feel some elation
It's you and the water
And your inhalation

It's you and the water
It's you blowing bubbles
Exhaling the air
Releasing your troubles
To be there in water
Is a natural thing
You can mumble and curse
Or just start to sing

It knows who you are
It knows how you feel
It tells you right now
It shows you it's real
There's magic in water
It is no illusion
Your body submerged
In this clear solution
It sings all around you
With glimmers of light
It is meditation
It's sight beyond sight

You feel quite reborn
In this pool of water
When it's cold at the start
And then becomes hotter
The water remembers
You were there once before
You were there many times
It knows to keep score

It speaks what you feel
If you're gentle or kind
If you're rough on the edges
Or of clear lucid mind
If the liquid is tough
If you cut through like butter
So much can be learned
While swimming in water

~

# The Realm of the Faceless

By

Omer Toledano


One day I will wake up

I will wake up from this dream

And see your true face

Your true nature

One day I will shed this mortal coil

This mortal toil

And then I will come to know

Your true being

I know who you are

You have always been there

The spinning globe

The sun rising in the east

Life sings its song

And You are here

With a blast of your nostrils

You move mountains

Please remove the veil

There is nothing left for me here

The Jig is up

I am close

Take my hand and pull me up

Sit me among the sea

Of forgotten souls

Let me look upon thy face

Let me look away

In the realm of the faceless

~

# Infinity Code

By

Omer Toledano

It began with the light
So that we all could see
Him in the self
And you in the me
It started off clean
What was
Was what is
And continued and grew
What is mine is now his
The fruit from the trees
The honey from bees
Man is now ruler
Does whatever he please

Unless he does not

Go forth

Do some cleaning

He will never achieve

To understand the true meaning

He has lost his direction

He must make a correction

And cease to make splits

Into section and section

There is only one

There is no division

What he knows to be true

Has distorted his vision

This is his moment

A short time for laughter

For eternity spans there

Both before and then after

No use for attachment
It is all for rent
The house that you live in
Your car's side dent
And even your body
Will once wither away
And give room to another
And a brand new day
All you must do
Is remember that you
Are a part of the fabric
In all that you do
Who you see and you love
Is sent from above
To show you who you are
And what you are made of
Till we meet I give you
A blessing forever
A blessing for now
And a blessing for never

Please accept all that is

In this type of mode

And help me to write

My infinity code

~

# Dance of Eternity

By

Omer Toledano


They've been dancing for years

Swaying for hours

Residing in silence

Presiding with powers

Clouds in formations

Rising of nations

Kings of the realm

Mad men at the helm

Up and down

And love comes to town

And then it comes closer

And off comes your gown

Then one day when you leave
I then sicken and heave
It then goes away
A storm, light of day
Consumed all by fire
And a loss of desire
It twists and then turns
Up in flames it burns
Delusions and visions
Human divisions
Physics in motion
Exchange of emotion
A heart beats in darkness
And the dark does not win
In the dance of eternity
You are out or you're in

~

# The Magical Mule

By

Omer Toledano


The Magical Mule is one to behold

He is sharp, he is wise

He is strong and he's bold

The Magical Mule never gives up

He never surrenders

He is quite a chump

Day in and day out

He pulls his load

He treads alone

This lonely road

The Magical Mule cannot complain

If he's feeling ill

Or if he's in pain

It matters not

To his masters on Earth

The Magical Mule

Is both blessed and cursed

On the one hand he's blessed

For he's made a living

On the other he's cursed

No life and just giving

Who now weeps for this Magical Mule

Who has left this world

A shiny jewel

Who will care for this mule

In a hundred years' time

Who will remember his face

And know who he was

Just a Magical Mule

Who did not make a fuss

Who followed one rule

For he knows who he was

In every sense of the word

A Magical Mule

~

# The Seed of Intention

By

Omer Toledano


There are things in this world

Beyond comprehension

Like time and its flow

With the seed of intention

You decide who you are

In each passing moment

What role do you play?

Is it joy or just torment?

Infinite wisdom is at our disposal

To reject all at once

Or accept a proposal

It's a game, simulation

Every choice that we make

Whether high in the air

Or enjoying a lake

Ultimate truth at the heart of creation

A place that is still

Where all comes to cessation

Perpetual movements

Of body and mind

Come to a halt

And there you will find

The answer to that

Which you have been asking

The ultimate truth

Which you have been masking

It was there all along

You were too blind to see

Too busy sailing

This stormy sea

Before leaving again
One more thing I should mention
Plant it here, plant it now
Your seed of intention

~

# Autoresponse

By

Omer Toledano


The feeling is gone

I've lost the emotion

My current plea

A present notion

Maybe for the better

That I can no longer feel

That nothing has value

That it is no longer real

For others so simple

To trust

And cast meaning

So easy to fall

Against whom they are leaning

Time and again

It seems so obscure

All in its place

A magical cure

Like a program to start

To connect to the heart

To feel at the core

To open a door

Like a mouse in a lab

The yellow cab

Crosses the bridge

A metallic slab

A hotel in the city

A six year old boy

The world on his finger

To love and enjoy

I guess that is it
All that there is
Fading memories
Of all that is His
It is always the now
In all that was once
An empty reaction
An auto-response

~

# Equinox

By

Omer Toledano


Something to be said

About this fluctuation

Twice a year it occurs

In our Earthly rotation

Once in the Autumn

And once in the Spring

Masculine Feminine

It's a beautiful thing

It is not felt by many

They're not even aware

Do not know it exists

Do not know it is there

North and South become one

And the sun is aligned

Equal light to the poles

It's a wonderful ride

Male turns to Female

Female turns to Male

Complete equilibrium

In this solar sail

The Earth keeps on spinning

In a slight slanted axis

And we to new worlds

Begin to gain access

Once we are there

Once we are here

It all lasts for cycles

Of half a year

It goes on through the ages

Felt by Scientists and Sages

It spins like a quarter

Maintains cosmic order

Shows to us all

That space has no border

To the firm disbeliever

Who reads this and mocks

Whether you know it or not

It is now equinox

~

# Heartbeats & Seconds

By

Omer Toledano


The countdown begins

Refuse to bins

Throw the garbage away

And then second hand

Like grains of the sand

And the heart is trying to say

Heartbeat and second

Are in sync the boy reckoned

A purpose for every event

When time began

With a beat of his heart

And the motion to eternity sent

The world created with this vibration
It is sometimes well overlooked
For the rays of the sun
In his morning run
With the world this one is now hooked
Connected to all with umbilical cord
Which has never for once been severed
He is the Earth and the Sun and the Moon
A Nomad out in the desert
The air he breathes in and the blood in his veins
Constructions, a weak explanation
For they matter not in this house of delights
And they surely pose no limitation
Seduction of spirit is all there is here
And the mind is trying to bind you
With a backdrop for life
A flute and a fife
Look ahead and not what's behind you

A heartbeat a second

"Come with me!" the boy beckoned

What more evidence do you require?

I will carry your burden and ease your pain

Let me be your formidable squire

Where we go from here

In your hands it will be

As it has been right from the start

The hours and seconds will continue to pass

With the beating of your loving heart

~

# In Memoriam

By

Omer Toledano

Please remember
That I was once your son
That once I filled your world
With wonder and delight
That once I was the center
That once I was alright
Please remember
That once I was your brother
Aggressive when I must
And only because once
In you I could not trust

Please remember

That I was once your friend

I saw myself in you

And you o' friend of mine

Saw the best in me

And let my spirit shine

Please remember

That I was once your lover

You showed me

What it means to love

To lose myself there in another

And you

Will you remember who you were

When all of this is gone

Will you remember anything

When all of this is done

Please remember everything

There is no good or bad

Your light shines to eternity

And nothing you once had

Nothing to take with you

No meat, no skin, no bone

For when time comes and comes to pass

To there you go alone

No memory of anything

Of you who is no more

It was all a test I put you through

To guide you to the door

Rest in peace o' child of mine
While walking through a garden
And know that you are here with me
Alone but not forgotten

~

# The Servant

By

Omer Toledano

Leave me to dwell in your presence, divine one

Embrace me with your silence and eternal wisdom

Let me see through your eyes

The timeless melody of your unbounded song

Free me once more from this web of deception

So that I may once more empty myself of this deluge of delusion

And find your path through the storm

Which you in your infinite wisdom

Have manifested with your mighty hand

To keep me from seeing the true intention of your divine will

Find me once more o' great one

You know where I am

In purity will you come to know my intention

In beauty will you come to know my everlasting love

In truth will you come to know my way

There is no other

We are one

Your heart's echoing cry has brought me to you once again

And there I shall remain

Your servant

For all eternity

~

# Shadow

By

Omer Toledano


A wintry night

Black & mysterious

Cold & damp

Kid you not

I am serious

Whispering winds

Telling tales of long past

Floods and showers

How long will they last?

Sing me a song

Young maiden in yellow

Know me to sleep

Kiss this young-looking fellow

Where have they gone

Those sirens of old?

Why must I stand here out in the cold?

Come here young lady

To have and to hold

Till death do us part

On mountains of gold

This is my shadow

It is him so I'm told

Stand up straight

Stand up tall

Stand up strong

Stand up bold

Why must you stand there

You there in the back

Where is your light

That you desperately lack

What is your purpose

Who do you serve

Do you reap what you sow

And what you deserve

You are my shadow

You are me in the dark

If I was a fish

Why then you'd be a shark

We are one in the same

And we constantly fight

You in the dark

And me in the light

~

27569199R00049